Taste
of
Wonder

Poems of Hope
for Dark Times

LUKAS IRIZARRY

WESTBOW
PRESS®
A DIVISION OF THOMAS NELSON
& ZONDERVAN

Author photo Cara Sandford

WestBow Press books may be ordered through booksellers or by contacting:

WestBow Press
A Division of Thomas Nelson & Zondervan
1663 Liberty Drive
Bloomington, IN 47403
www.westbowpress.com
1 (866) 928-1240

ISBN: 978-1-5127-9858-6 (sc)
ISBN: 978-1-5127-9856-2 (hc)
ISBN: 978-1-5127-9857-9 (e)

Library of Congress Control Number: 2017912644

Print information available on the last page.

WestBow Press rev. date: 09/18/2017

To my family, who has always held me up
and fanned the flames of my wonder.

To Mom, Dad, Nathan, Marlena, and Arlen.
You have always held me up and
fanned the flames of my wonder.

To Jake, Jess, Katrina, Jim, Deb, Heidi, Pete, and
Annabelle. You were with me in the darkest times.

To Tom, Brandon, and Mike, my eternal friends.

I love you all. Thank you for everything.

Introduction

God's call isn't always a pleasant one. The following poems are memories of prayers where God kept me going through depression. They echo the eternal grace and love that inspired them. I hope that they will help you through your difficult times as well.

To paraphrase Ravi Zacharias: If you receive any good from this book, then thank God. If you find any mistakes, then thank me.

Relationships

I Apologize

During a transition between career paths, I served as a youth pastor. I certainly felt called to it and filled a necessary gap in that particular church's staff, temporarily. However, I was keenly convicted regarding facets of my personality that needed improvement. I longed to be a more perfect version of myself before I was touted as a "leader."

As I grew up in church, I became more and more struck by the duplicity of some members of my home church. This experience coupled with the increasing difficulty of living a Christian life in a secular world left me impassioned to bring a no-nonsense message to my youth audience. My students continually encountered real-life issues of drugs, depression, sex, and suicide that were outside the realms of polite church curriculum. Additionally, some parents wanted more curriculum and less personal talk. Some wanted more lessons and less game time. Everybody has an opinion when they're outside the arena. This poem is for both my students and the parents. It expresses my insufficiency, fear, calling, and ultimate purpose in being a shepherd for that small flock.

I apologize;
I'm an evil person trying to do good.
I apologize

If I never really ever do as good as I should.
I apologize;
I've seen the Lord, the Risen Lamb.
I apologize
If I don't look like who He says I am.

I'm really sorry
If my words seem unsafe;
I'm really sorry
For the difference between doctrine
And my walk in the faith.
I'm really sorry
If my feelings seem real,
But I'm not sorry
My real wounds have been healed.

I do regret it
That I have led some astray.
I do regret it
That they took serious what I meant for play.
I do regret it
That leadership bears a heavy burden.
I do regret it
That I'm only a fragile vessel, earthen.

My Lord is good, though;
Maybe you've heard.
My Lord is good, though;
You can take Him at His word.
My Lord is good, though;
He'll see you through.
My Lord is good, though;
He'll make you new.

So here I am,
Imperfect messenger.
Here I am,
Redeemed inheritor.
Here I am,
At the behest of my Lord.
Here I am,
Not of my own accord.

What will you do
With words that I bring?
What will you do
With the song that I sing?
What will you do,
Young student of mine?
What will you do
With my words and my time?

Given by God,
They express me most deeply.
Given by God,
They confess me most freely.
Redeemed by God,
I'm no perfect specimen,
Chosen by God
To act as good medicine.

I point to the Father
Through the Son, Jesus Christ.
I point to the Father
Through the man who lived twice.
I point to the Father

Through my sinful bones;
I point to the Father
'Cause Christ brought me home.

My dear mortal kin,
He's calling you too.
My dear mortal kin,
He loves you through and through.
My dear mortal kin,
Time's running short.
My dear mortal kin,
Pursue Him and do not abort.

To His person and death,
There's but one response—
To His person and death,
Which source life-giving fonts.
His person and death
Bound you and I.
His person and death
Enthroned Him on high.

The time's almost up;
Do you know you're forgiven?
The time's almost up;
Will you continue sinning?
The time's almost up,
And Christ will return.
The time's almost up;
Where will you go when it is your turn?

Heaven's Tears

$\mathcal{M}$any people in my life are already saved, but there are a few people in my life who I desperately want to see in heaven. For these individuals my heart especially longs since I have known them for some time. Sometimes I wonder if they'll make it, and it hurts me. It is a pain that I know is felt throughout all heaven as well.

> Heaven, cry through me
> Tears like the sea.
> Weep and wail
> Along this dusty trail;
> The straight and narrow
> Shakes me to my marrow.
> Thorns on my shins
> Bleed me of my sins;
> By His stripes we're healed,
> By His spirit sealed.
> Love eternal,
> God paternal,
> Where is home?
> Past the star's dome,
> Far away.
> I cannot stay;

My heart longs.
I write songs
For friends of old,
Their stories told.
Don't forget them,
But I don't expect them.
Prove me wrong.
Prove You're strong,
To bring them home
'Yond the starry dome.

The tears of heaven
Flow half-past eleven
Beneath the starry dome.
Beneath the starry dome,
Half-past eleven,
For those who aren't yet home.

Intro to Compassion

*O*f the spiritual disciplines, compassion is one of the most difficult. The etymology breaks down into "com," meaning "with," and "passion," meaning "pain." To step outside yourself into someone else's pain is an act of sacrifice. It requires love, because there is no other motivator that will lead us to choose pain for ourselves (with no apparent reward) when we could have chosen comfort.

I was also musing over the function that poetry has in my own life. The flow of the words and construction of the verse add layers beyond basic communication. So it seems it is a powerful way to explore the realms of imagination.

Poetry in spirit swings
To bring about new and glad tidings,
To make known something new,
Something which prose simply cannot do.

The secrets of the spirit's wonder
Are in silent realms a-slumber,
To be woken by blessed rhyme.
And not a moment before their time

Do you feel its call and certain rhythm
Surfing between the dimensional schism?
It is what's certain and certainly relevant
To wake your soul from cloudy tenement.

Look around and see what glistens;
Begin to use your mind to listen.
Feel the waves of certain sorrow;
Do not try to predict tomorrow.

The certain sorrow in people down,
They give off vibes like trumpet sounds.
When you notice their mood without a word,
You'll realize it's their souls you've heard.

Step two, step back and take a listen
To someone ambitious and on a mission.
Hear their hard and poignant words
And how their soul inside them curds.

For peace and rest and love abundant,
They've traded that for wealth incumbent.
Now where to? They cannot see,
So they waste another year for more money.

Now to loved ones hark and learn;
To their hearts your senses turn.
Feel their light and love so strong
From those to whom you could do no wrong.

This life and love divine—
When you feel it, waste no time
On fights, distractions, or petty strife.
Simply give and take delight.

Step four is yours only if you're ready,
And if your intuition's steady.
Take a look inward—what do you see?
Why, everyone's problems are also in me.

Evangelisto

$\mathcal{I}$t's easy to forget the true reason why the church is here on earth: to make disciples. Maybe it's because I've been in the church my whole life, or maybe it's because I'm a sinful man who wants to ignore the call of Christ when it suits my sinful nature. We are called to pour out our hearts to others repeatedly, to tell them of the intimate wonders of Jesus Christ and the blessings that He's stored up for us. And then we must go back to Him to be refilled time and time again. Evangelism is exhausting.

Those moments of exhaustion allow the sinful nature in us to creep out if we are not vigilant. When the spirit is tired, the body starts looking for trouble. But even in those moments when our spirit is weary, God's spirit never tires. He seeks us, finds us, and meets us right where we are with understanding, not condemnation. He is our high priest who can sympathize with our every trial (Hebrews 4:15).

A weary man stood
On the streets of Babylon.
He had been sent here quickly
From the land beyond.
Born again he was
And given a new name.

He was sent to carry a message
And relieve the people of their shame.

He stood on the corner
And called for repentance.
An act like this was punishable
With severe sentence,
But so few had listened
Or even taken interest
That he began to feel that his mission
And Master were just a little bit senseless.

Day after day, year after year,
Our weary man from the land beyond
Stood right on the corner here.
The men walked by and jeered;
The women strolled by and teased him.
There were so few reliefs in this city,
Less that would ever please him.

But one day he grew tired, like so many others.
A temptation took hold,
As it had for so many of his brothers.
"Just a little won't hurt," he said so sure.
It was now five o'clock;
A drink of spirit might be the cure.

So he drifted and dodged
As if someone would follow,
But with every step he took,
He felt a little more hollow.
The temptations of Babylon

Had hit him just right,
And now he stood at the doors
Of the entrance to the night.

"Happy hour 5–7,"
Read the bright sign in neon.
This was one of those places
From which your best friends hastened thee on.
But in did he walk.
He found vices and then some.
He found drinks and drugs
And people having their "fun."

He walked up to the bar and said,
"I'll have one drink."
The bartender looked and said,
"Here's a man who doesn't want to think."
Indeed, he was right.
Our man was ashamed.
He had given up his mission
For the drink that defamed.

"Well, here's your first offering.
Come back for a second."
In five minute the man did
Just as the barkeep beckoned.
Now at the brim of his third, his head began to swirl.
He'd not drank in some time—
His stomach began to curdle.

The barkeep eyed him and said, "Are you okay?"
The man recovered and said,

"Here's what I have to say!
I stand on the streets,
And all I do is yell
About how all of you people
Are going straight to hell!
It's eternal punishment,
And you don't seem to care
That I'm giving you the one way
To get someplace more fair.

"No one seems to listen,
And I'm getting quite sick of it.
Do you know what it's like
Being right in the thick of it?
Through snow and through sleet
I've been chasing tired souls,
Yet they choose to be here
In this dirty, rotten hole."

The crowd had turned to hear him,
But when he was done,
They turned back to their vices.
They turned back to their fun.
"And what about you?"
The man spoke to the barkeep.
"You feed them their swill.
I wonder how your conscience speaks."
The barkeep just smiled
And kept cleaning a glass.
Then light bounced off his chest,
Off something like brass.

The man took a look
And for the first time could see
That the barkeeper's nametag said,
"Jesus of Galilee."

Our pastor began to tremble as
The barkeep approached.
He said, deep and tender,
"My heart is beyond reproach.
Those sitting behind you
Were tempted to flee their conscience.
They were moved by your sermons,
Yes, even the staunchest.
Because of you, they got to meet me directly."
The man said through tears,
"But they all look so messy."
Jesus chuckled with love in his eyes.
"I remember a time when you looked just like
any one of these guys."

The pastor began to weep,
Though he tried to hold back.
What felt to him a failure
Had been success—that's a fact.
The Word of God goes out
And never comes back empty.
Our weakness is His strength;
Our lacking is His plenty.

"I still don't get it. Why do you allow vice?"
Jesus answered, "At first I could not,
Until I made a great sacrifice.

Now I work and watch, offering them living water,
And then I point them my way
When they ask, 'Where's the Father?'"

The pastor was in wonder,
But something wasn't clear.
"What you served me was not water.
It was, in fact, beer."
Jesus raised an eyebrow. "This is my bar.
What I serve is my choice.
But note that what you drank
Brought out your true voice.
How long has it been
Since you've been honest with me?
Have you forgotten
That your whole heart I can see?"
The pastor smiled and marveled at this man
Who watched the chaos behind him
As if it were all part of a plan.

"Will they ever be clean? I just have to know,"
The pastor asked Jesus. "Yes—whiter than snow.
What you see is a process, and it's not quite yet over.
Oh, but when it is, they'll shine bright
and smell sweeter than clover."

The man sighed in relief.
"I guess you've got them covered."
Jesus replied, "More than you know,
My enduring, kind brother.
Now finish your portion of ferment and foam.
Finish your drinks, and I'll take you home."

Walking in the World

A Prayer for a City

$\mathcal{I}$ cared very deeply for the town in which I went to college. There were very many bright souls who walked from class to class with me. But they were suppressed due to the natural temptations of college: drinking, smoking, and sleeping around. The wares of the world were dropped on them with phrases like, "You have the right to be whoever you want to be." This justification is supposed to come through the saving grace of Christ. But, as usual, the world has taken things that belong to God, repackaged them, and sold them for profit to the loss of its consumers. I could imagine demons sitting on the fences of that school. They jeered at and mocked the crowds. They laughed at the listless wandering of the souls. They laughed harder at those who went so deep that they wondered if their lives had any meaning or purpose.

This morning, I cried and broke down a little.
My words were filled with grief and spittle.
I looked for God and found Him not—
Just a whisper from beyond my thought.

Why do you leave me in this broken plane?
Why do you let me feel this pain?
Does this place have any sense,

19

Where demons jeer from on the fence,
That keeps in prison priceless souls
And drives them into fraternity's holes,
Where parties drive and communities cease,
Where turbulence overcomes all peace,
Where snow and light and natural wonder
Are replaced by drunken intentional blunder?

I sit beside a withered tree,
Wondering, "Will my efforts come back to me?"
I rail against God, a natural Jonah,
While I watch, repenting, those of Ninevah.

My attitude is sour
As I repeat every hour,
"God, I could use a display of your power."

I await the time
And await the place
Where demons, by angels, are given chase

To see these people
Finally set free
And when home will be delivered to me.

Pain

So much stuff has gone awry,
So many reasons to ask why.
If there's God, then why's there pain?
But you don't know sun till you've seen rain.

My God, my God, why have you forsaken?
Deep down I know, a pure heart you're makin'
Expectations of perfection have left me high and dry.
Luckily, my God is faithful—humanity's *semper fi.*

Days of Noah

Goodness gracious,
Well I'll be!
It's a different time, you see,
When girls will be boys
And boys will be girls.
How much more nonsense until the skies uncurl?

Gender's not the issue,
It's the heart of man
Who thinks he/she can succeed within his or her own plan.
It's a little bit funny
But kind of intense
That people believe that they can be "on the fence."

Up on the fence
Is still down in hell,
And that will be the place that you eternally dwell.
Come out of the gates
Into His wide arms.
The time is short; you must be alarmed.

This is fair warning.
This is fair play.
I hope we will all be together someday.
Heaven is better,
And hell is far worse,
So excuse me, dear friend, if my words seem terse.

The stakes are high,
And the risks are abundant.
To not make a choice is damnation incumbent.
I'm nervous for you
Every day.
I can't bear the thought of our souls torn away.

November 7, 2016

'Twas the night before voting,
And not a creature was stirring.
The whole nation was tense—
Historic days were unfurling.
One little vote,
Just some ink on a paper,
Will change our great nation
Both now and for later.
But as the people stewed,
There remained one more choice.
It was a pressing matter
To which media had not given voice.
Two matters are at hand,
Though too few will attend.
Many are too worried
Believing that this is the end.
"One nation, under God"
Is how I was raised,
To love on my neighbor
Is how God was praised.
Yet people use politics
To hate on their brother,
And no one's concerned

About anyone other
Than their candidate, their first pick,
Their choice of the draft,
And this is how the whole nation
Ended up daft.
The government's not the end
Of your or my life,
So stop letting it cause
So much cruel strife.
The day after tomorrow,
It's all back to business.
We'll no longer debate
Who is going to win this.
But we'll have our family, spouses,
Co-workers, and friends,
And I reckon a few of us
Will have to make amends.
See, this nation is great
Because we refuse to be divided
By government, by politics,
By words that have derided.
Americans are good,
And generous too.
This I believe in my heart
All the way through.
So tomorrow we all have
Two choices to make:
To reach out to brothers and sisters
Or give in to hate.
So go on and pick
Your favorite worst option,
But be on your guard—

Don't let bad thoughts come in.
It's really a child's lesson,
But we need it right now
Because if this nation falls,
Then this will be how.
Despite your chosen party,
Go fight the good fight.
When given an option and facing darkness,
Choose light.

Joy

The proceedings of the 2016 presidential election were troubling. The corruption exposed on both sides really only mirrored the corruption that swept across the American spirit. To see it in its full form was sickening. I prayed that this would not be the end of the country. I prayed that darkness would be overcome with light. I feared that darkness; it seemed so strong. I was quickly reprimanded and reminded of who has the true power.

> For they in whom the spirit weeps,
> Those who fill the crowded streets,
> To they to whom the Son of God speaks,
> Lament.
>
> To those who hear on the western wind
> The voice of He who died for sin,
> The family of Christ (who died for all),
> Lament.
>
> Make use of your voice and raise a call
> Within your houses and fellowship halls.
> Wake up the night with tears and moans.
> Lament.

Make haste, undress, and lie on the ground.
Be still and silent, and don't make a sound.
Weep the cause of our distress.
Lament.

When terror strikes and darkness nears,
Make sure your cries reach God's ears.
He listens close to those in tears.
Lament.

Why, oh why, my God, my God, did you let us fall apart?
Why, oh why, my Lord, my Lord, did
you let evil gain the start?
"Peace, be still, I'm with you here.
Be my light in so much fear.
Take all your hope and shine it forth.
Guide the lost like the star of the north."

My God, my God, but don't you hear?
There's so much evil afoot down here.
Corruption holds the highest tier;
It seems as if no good draws near.

"I'm close right here and close afar.
I rule the earth and all the stars.
Since time long past, I've been around.
Remember, it's Me who made the ground.

"Fear not the ones who play charades,
Who write bad laws behind colonnades.
Fear not the emperors and kings amiss,
For none exist against my wish.

"I put kings up and I put them down.
I exalt the lowly and replace the clown.
I make right all things that have gone wrong.
I take as a joke those who are strong.

"So laugh and giggle at tyrants in play.
Don't forget I'm coming back someday
To judge the just and wicked alike,
To separate darkness from the light.

"So serve for now, my little child.
I've sent you out as sheep so mild.
Fear not the wolves and serpents strong;
I keep abreast of who does wrong.

"If I care for you, what does it mean
If an evil person builds scheme on scheme?
All efforts fail, and weapons rust.
Against my Word they turn to dust.

"The plans and means of those in power,
Are leases lent soon to go sour.
The jig is up; I still preside.
I'm glad to have you on my side."

At this I wept no longer more,
After hearing such sweet words from my Lord.
Taken aback and comforted sweet,
I laid my head gently down to sleep.

Shorts

*O*ccasionally I write personal thoughts in short poems. Here are a few.

The Insubstantiality of Success

I choked on mountain air too thin.
I tried so hard, but I couldn't win.
All the dreams stashed up
I couldn't reach.
I'm a general in rags,
A leader impeached.
I fought so hard and became so brittle.
For all of my efforts the return is so little.

On the Strength of Love

Love is strong,
Far stronger than war.
To take up the sword
I've a million reasons or more.
But to put it back down
I've reasons few,
Excepting divine grace
To forgive you.

Faith v. Fun

The future is now.
You can grasp it and hold it,
But you will never see it.
The past is yet to come.
Chase it, drink it, smoke it.
You'll see it, but only come so close.

Personal Folly

I am too weak to admit weakness,
So I appear strong and pray you'll play along.
I am too lean to be mean,
So I act tough and pray that that's enough.
I am too wrong to admit I'm wrong,
So I force my way and fasten my will strong.
I am too petty to admit I'm petty,
So I chase fortune like confetti.
I'm so much fluff that I've seen I'm fluff;
I earnestly beg God to be made of sterner stuff.

On Patience and Persistence

They have no allure, but the reward is great—
The best things come to those who wait.
Temptation tries, and weak flesh wails,
But against King on high, all darkness fails.

Written During a Sunset on the Beach

Season's greeting,
Old friends meeting.
Time is passing,
Waves are crashing,
Toils hard
And struggles tight.
I only survive
By His might.
Waves are crashing,
Bad things are passing.
In Christ we're fraternal,
And all good things are eternal.

On Nightmares

My life is gone.
My strength has left my bones.
My leaping heart of hope and joy
Is dry and desolate stone.

My God has left
And allowed this terror.
I hoped and dreamed that life would spring
And turn out all the fairer.

Romans 5:28:
Things turn out all right.
But my heart is wrecked, and I twist and turn,
Trying to love away all this fright.

Graduation as a Movie

Sitting atop a campus spire,
Only a few weeks until I retire.
It took a lot of work to get me here;
I faced demons and felt some fear.
It wasn't just me who labored hard;
My family and friends were casted stars.
Where does it all go from here?
Not important—I'm soaking up good cheer.
Here's to a moment that's pretty great.
Here's to the God of my eternal fate.

Where to Put Your Problems

No person can bear your weakness.
This will make you stronger—
When you let go to Jesus,
He'll hold on even longer.

Sin and Vice

Wake-Up Call

Originally, I pursued science instead of art. It was a definite and secure future, as far as I could tell. There was money and possibly fame if I ever made any sort of discovery. One morning I was dealing with wild uncertainty regarding my future. I complained to God about the waves around me while walking on the water of a life I never planned on. He responded:

"Your riches and your fame,
You'll be fine without it.
I've got you covered from dawn to dusk.
Don't ever try to doubt it.

"You speak too much and listen too little.
My words don't reach your ears.
You fret and fray and bustle and play
But never address your fears.

"Do you think it's life to never win,
To be held captive to your sin?
Do you call it 'good' when pleasures abound
But there's no salvation to be found?

"What's this life, this trick of yours?
Do you think it impresses me?
I made stars and seas and waves;
I crafted galaxies.

"Give it up, and come and see
Just what I have in store.
Come, give it up, and come and see.
I promise there's so much more.

"The world is lost, and you're not home.
Your life's an empty throne.
The world is lost, and you fritter away
On your computer and your phone.

"But my home is large, with rooms for you all—
I've a mansion for you and your friends.
My Father is waiting; the angels are eager
To welcome you. I've made amends."

Riches

Another day, another dollar,
But the riches make me smaller.
How many millions of dollars
Would erase earth's sinful squalor?

All the world's pleasures
And all of Satan's measures
Are trying to rob me of my heavenly treasures.

When I get to slipping,
When I get to tripping,
I learn more and more how the Holy Cross is fitting.

My sin on a tree:
My God died for me,
Savior of the world hung where everybody could see.

Shame of the world,
Glory to be unfurled,
Cross on his back and bloody fingers knurled,

Passion in unbroken bones,
Glory is His throne.
Soon He's coming back, someday,
To take His people home.

A Bad Idea

I was inspired by C. S. Lewis's *Screwtape Letters*. So I imagined a modern scenario of demons plotting the demise of the souls of young people. In this particular instance, I was at the gym. Everyone had their headphones in, but I wondered what else they heard every time they looked in the mirror. What darts did Satan shoot into their minds regularly?

"I have an idea,"
Said a demon to his peers.
"It'll keep us entertained
For the next fifty years.
We'll tell the men to get muscular
To cover up their fears,
And tell the women to get skinny—
Then they'll have no more tears.
And when they come around
To see they're ugly and worn,
We'll have filled up their hearts
With self-hatred and scorn.
'Why can't I find happiness
In my physical form?'
It's a practical joke!
We'll laugh as they mourn."

"I think I have a plan,"
Said a demon to his peers.
"On this much pain, we'll get drunk
When people's cries reach our ears.

"Have all the actors,
and actresses too,
Make people believe that their
Dreams will come true.
'Just believe in yourself.
There's no work to do,
Cause no one in the world
Is more special than you.'
We'll dance and we'll sing
Around their collective oppression,
Then hide behind medicine
and call it depression.

"Keep them from making
that one true confession.
Distraction and confusion
Is the point of our profession.

"I've got an idea—
Now lean in and listen,
Cause this might just be
The fulfillment of our mission.
But wait, here He comes!
Oh my, how He glistens.
It really is a shame that He knows what we're wishin'.'"

Along came a man,
Gleaming and bright.
He came through and ruined
The demons' dark night.
With short and terse words,
He dispelled all their scheming
By reminding them of people
And their heavenly meaning.

"Who do you think you are,
And who said you could speak?
Cause I believe that I died
To bring home my sheep.

"Now, my name is Jesus.
I don't know if you've heard—
Long before creation,
They just called me the Word.

"I came to bring a sword,
So I hope it's plain to see
That no force in creation
Is above my decree.
Your plans and your schemes,
They don't frighten me
Cause I came to this earth
To set my people free!

"Your temporary distractions
And your hopes of destruction
Will not get in the way
Of my church's construction.

"So get up off my daughter,
And get away from my son.
You have no authority,
And the battle is won."

Why Do I Do When I Do Not Want? (or Romans 7)

If Jesus saved me from my sin, then I shouldn't sin, right? Like so much of life, the actual outworking of the idea of salvation is complex. It has facets, nooks, and crannies where dark aspects of our souls and flesh cling to existence. Even these must be fought and removed from our being. Jesus' spirit wrestles within us to clean us. We must also fight as the spirit leads. The necessity of this fight frustrated me because I always figured Jesus could make it go away with a single word. But for whatever divine reason, He hasn't. And it is not for the clay to ask the potter, "Why are you doing this?"

Paul beautifully illustrates the believer's struggle against sin in Romans 7. His constant back-and-forth with his sinful nature gives the most enlightened view into the soul of the believer. Paul also outlines the final hope that the believer has in Jesus Christ.

> Endless thoughts and pains forgiven
> In my mind where I'm always sinnin'—
> Protect me, please, oh Savior God,
> From these weary plains I trod.

Keep me in peace and perfect silence.
Till I come home, keep me from violence.
Sometimes in anger I do swell,
But from no source that friends could tell.
I can't see why, though I'm forgiven,
I must continue so gladly sinnin'.

I know I'm saved—that's pretty great—
So why, oh why, can I conjure hate?
Your blood covers me and washes clean.
Then why on earth can I be so mean?

Were you sick of yourself?
Did you ever feel it?
That gnawing lurch, you can't conceal it?
Hebrews says you understand,
But the gospels say you're a perfect man.
Was there sin in your flesh that you had to wrestle?
Were you bad to the bone, to your body's trestle?

How did you sustain and maintain, not complain?
Sometimes I can't stand the sound of my own name.
Just keep me close and don't let me do it.
God, how on earth did you make it through it?

Elect?

$\mathcal{T}$he problem with depression is that it can sink so far into your soul that it makes you question your salvation. "How could I be saved if I feel like this?" Paul himself talks about despairing of life. So even though I felt forgotten by God, it seemed to be a pointless feeling to entertain because so many of God's children endured that despair. Paul despaired of life, Jesus sweat blood in the garden, Noah became drunk, and the prophet Elijah was so exhausted from his fight with the prophets of Baal that he prayed for God to kill him. The Bible is full of stories of God's people who have suffered deep darkness in their lives, but God rescues them all.

Truth in story,
Truth in science,
Both are seeking your compliance.
Fear in doubt,
Strength in wonder,
The force of each will tear asunder.
Love by sight and
Love by choice,
Love eternal with your own voice,
Taken by force and
Given by will,

This time I drink my sinful swill.
All I've gained
And all I've lost
Are nothing but the garbage tossed.
Does it matter
What choice I make
If it doesn't put my soul at stake?
Can I work through
This eternal pain
And make it back to heaven again?
Am I damned
To my own fate,
Or will God open up the gate?

My own fate
I cannot stand;
It makes me feel
The reprimand.
Can I be ground
Into flying?
Is it possible?
My soul is trying.
My childhood joy
I remember clear;
I would employ it
And keep it near.
Cause my dreams and hope,
They've gone awry.
I can no longer see the sky.
God took away
My salvation;
I cannot enjoy

His own creation.
There is no pleasure
Without His favor,
Without His smiling face to savor.
This is death
While I'm alive.
I do not think
I can survive.
Pleasure is a mercy
To help contend
With eternal winter that will not end.
Am I elect,
Or am I damned?
Either way, it's what God has planned.
Yes, indeed, it's what God has planned.

Spiritual Walk

Head Games

Oh Lord on high,
I miss your presence nigh.
My thoughts slip away from me like a thief, sly.

Your spirit inside me,
Your myst'ries confide in me.
Is this your bidding, 'fore I stand beside thee?

I'll pour out your wisdom
And know more of your kingdom,
Salt all of my words and make my arguments winsome.

Your truth and your grace
Have a singular face
With whose mercy and love I cannot keep pace.

Short work of my sin
I know you will win.
You had my course set before time did begin.

All of my thoughts,
The works I have wrought—
I hope to your face a smile they have brought.

As you continue
From heavenly venue,
From down here on earth my prayers I'll send you.

Don't forget me
When you come to see
Who's done your bidding and has believed thee.

Don't forget me
When you come to see
Who's done your bidding and has become free.

From hell that entangles
And dark sin that mangles,
Who's obeyed your spirit and bowed as he wrangles

Your spirit kinetic,
So powerful, energetic.
Finish your love's circuit; in me please connect it.

He who leads without word
In my heart He has stirred
And brought me in line with the rest of your herd.

The good shepherd Jesus
Continually frees us.
We're vapors in the wind, but He acts like He needs us.

Where did it come from?
You're perfect and then some.
You take note of me, a dog eating breadcrumbs.

Oh author of life,
The church as your wife
Cut through this dark world like a flaming red knife.

With sword from your mouth
You ride from heaven, south.
You sweep through the nations, your enemies to rout.

Though my motives are clashin',
You quell all my passion
And dress me in robes after Your heavenly fashion.

Take pain away,
Oh dear Lord, I pray.
Make it happen quick on your glorious day.

Time flows like sand,
The grains through my hand.
One thousand years in a day, I can't understand.

I watch my face age
On this earthly stage;
As I rail against passions, at my flesh do I rage.

It costs me my soul,
But You'll make me whole.
You'll redeem all the years that the locust stole.

Enthrone me in heaven;
Remove all my leaven.
Let me rest up like You on sabbath day seven.

My course you have set.
I'm willing to bet
The end will be glorious, but it's not over yet.

All of my time
Wrapped up in rhyme,
As I escape sin, heavenly mountains I climb.

Straight and Narrow

It's easy to rest in the eternal salvation of your soul. It's easy to believe there's no work left to do. However, Christ calls us onward to perfection, from glory to glory. There's work to be done, and the road can be difficult as bad habits are overcome and sin is conquered day by day.

Lord, I know you've gone ahead of me,
But my body won't agree.
Instead of living peaceably,
I'm filled with anxiety.

Lord, I know you took on the cross
My shame and guilt and dross.
The message I can't seem to get across
Is that your win's my flesh's loss.

The straight and narrow's tough right now.
I can feel the sweat upon my brow.
To die with you, I must allow
My flesh to burn, my knee to bow.

Don't get it wrong—I'm thankful, though.
You suffered pain I'll never know.

You took forty lashes and Roman blows
So I can walk on golden roads.

Please be patient as I start to live
And learn how deeply you forgive.
As I read daily your holy missive,
You let me survive the thresher's sieve.

What If?

I pondered one day on how life can take us in strange directions. I wondered how God uses this world to test us. I meditated on how what we want and what makes us happy seem to conflict.

What if self-confidence came
From doing things you set out to do?
What if happiness came
From investing in those who mean the most to you?
What if good health and comfort
Were goals and not givens,
And even when possessed
Of constitution like ribbons?
To be taken and broken in a moment without notice,
The winds of time spare no mercy for these delicate lotus.
What if purpose didn't come
From a magazine's advice,
But came from giving all
To be used as God's device?
What if on earth and in time
Is not where we're meant for?
And we're just passers-by
On a journey eternal.

What if our brief stay
In the dark and in the cold—
What if all our time spent
Becoming more old—
Were precursors to something
A whole lot more wondrous?
What if all our lives' trials
Aided our mortalities' slow undress?
What if the whispers from beyond
Both time and space
Found their most blessed utterance
From a familiar face
Of much debate
And controversy?
Yes, I do believe fully,
Undoubtedly, it's He,
Jesus Christ, the God-man,
The Lion and the Lamb,
Gently issuing comfort that He's got a plan,
That this life's the preface
To a world more becoming,
A world more fit to express
What keeps your heart thrumming,
An artist's ultimate dream
And a warrior's true test,
A musician's greatest song
And the traveler's final rest,
A home for the weary
And a place made by love,
A place not in space
But somewhere above.

Hang on, fellow pilgrim—
Take each moment with grace,
And look forward each moment
To when you see Him face-to-face.

Ascent

After a long battle and the end of one chapter of life, I looked forward to a much-needed repose.

Holy Spirit's taken off.
I hear crowds mock and jeer and scoff
As I take flight.
They want to fight,
As if the darkness overcomes the light,
As if the day would fear the night.

I rise above to realms unknown;
The scoffing fades to gentle drone.
I cannot hear it;
I do not fear it.
I'll rise above to where I clear it.
My destiny—the Lord will steer it.

Years of darkness overtaken,
I was stirred—a little shaken.
He kept me safe
From demon strafe.
By myself, I'd lose to the wraith,
But with His help I've kept the faith.

One episode I've overcome,
But now I know my life's not done.
I take repose
Because God knows
The tide of battle ebbs and flows.
The tide recedes, and Jesus shows.

Take my mark; it is not mine.
It's the cross of my holy Savior—fine.
Sometimes it's heavy,
Sometimes unsteady.
The world and hell with insults levy,
But God won't let go till your mansion's ready.

"Take my heart, and let it be
Consecrated, Lord, to thee."
Make me pure
Until you're sure
The weight of glory I can endure.
With stingless death, my sin you'll cure,
Part of your bride, your wife demure.
I pray more spirits will your blood procure
And souls heaven-bound your spirit lure.

Take my life, and let it be
Something that you're pleased to see.
My sin beguiles,
But your heart smiles
'Cause we'll dance on your Father's floor of tiles.
We can run on golden streets for miles.

I cannot wait to see you soon.
I know sometimes that I'm a goon.
I drop the ball
'Cause of the fall,
But on the cross you took it all
Because you love this heart so small.

The Mysteries

I often get frustrated in discussion with people who demand "proof" of God. They want God to perform like a circus clown or tamed lion, as if the heavens and earth weren't enough. God tells us not to test Him. He also told the Pharisees who demanded a sign that none would be given except the sign of Jonah (Matthew 12:39). But really the only reason I get frustrated is because I too lack faith and often demand a sign for this or that. It's easier to call the kettle black than to look in the mirror and see yourself quite rusty.

Here we go, another one —
A waking morning, battle won.
Yesterday's gone; tomorrow will come.
I'll conquer today by the power of the Son.

Call me Superman. I'm stronger than a planet.
When God comes near, my mind can hardly stand it.

All the earth and all its noise
Can barely make a scratch.
All creation waits in groaning
For the Sons of God to hatch.

Romans 1:16:
My cry, my creed, my anthem.
Second Corinthians 5:17:
The old me's just a phantom.
Psalm 23 is where I rest
And lay my head at night.
Ephesians 6:11–17
Prepares me for the fight.

Ezekiel contains the mysteries
That unzip your preconceptions.
Song of Solomon talks about that
Which rarely gets a mention.
Genesis 1 and Revelation
Tell of our King's reign;
Ecclesiastes and Lamentations
Are for when you're feeling off your game.

Now let me tell you a mystery, a very important verse,
A verse that puts the skeptic's
Religion neatly in its hearse:
"In the beginning God created ..."
The rest is said and done.
The rest of the chapter is
Where the heart of science gets its thrum.

The mathematical proof, as we know it today,
Is based on how Genesis 1 became arrayed.
You start and state your claim,
Then lay out your assumptions,
"Let there be light / let us make man"
Then a proof for your audience' consumption.

The proof herein is the one most glorious,
From Genesis on to John's vision euphorious.
Accept it by faith or just let it go,
But it will be far too late
By the time you can "know"
That our Savior's coming back because He's risen,
That to Him all authority has been given.

Battle Cry

Some artists derive inspiration from their dreams. I hope to get as far away from my nightmares as possible.

Bodies floating and trees on fire,
Such ideas nightmares inspire—
To take a world and watch it burn,
To hate a season and watch it turn.

Wretched people and wretched policy—
The ideal life seems solitary.
But it's not my calling, and not yours, either.
We're called to give the world a breather.

Take a world and watch it turn;
Tacit rotations I could spurn.
For heavenly peace I certainly yearn;
I guess I'll have to wait my turn

To shun my life to save another,
To love my enemy as my closest brother,
To pray for mild political weather,
To pray burdens lifted like a feather.

It's not fair, at least not yet,
To see others dry because I'm soaking wet.
I'll start to complain, and it's not pretty
To see my character so gritty.

I guess that's why it takes a lifetime
To quell this inner strife—mine.
Between my worst and His very best,
Sin weighs on me, a heavy vest.
But His glory's eternal and very bright.
God, give me strength to win the fight.

All the Different Churches

βetween Bible studies, children's ministries, youth group, drama team, worship team, media team, outreach, young adults' groups, young couples' groups, married couples' small groups, seniors' groups, and other missions, it can get easy to forget that Christ is the beginning and end of the mission. He is the fuel for the fire. It is good for a church to have many ministries, but not if that comes at the expense of people having a personal relationship with Christ. This is stated by Christ Himself in Revelation 1 and 2. In these passages, He calls the seven churches from sin, false teaching, and overworking back to a relationship with Himself.

I've seen a thousand different churches
Under a thousand different names.
They all met up on Sundays
Under steel and wooden frames,
Waiting for the preacher man
To go and tell his story,
Hoping that those wooden frames
Would take away their worry.
He said, "Now peace be with you,
And joy along your way,"

And then the joy has ended
An hour past midday.

I've seen a thousand different churches
With a thousand different names.
They are not corporate titles,
But "Bill" or "Beth" or "James."
They call their friends their siblings,
And their mentors are called mother.
All the while they stroll along
And forget their older brother,
Forgotten, blessed redeemer
Who died to make us new,
Crying out for conversation—
But we sit silent in a pew.

"My passion knows no bounds,
And my darkened past is glory.
My treasure is eternal,
But now it's gone a-whoring.
After friends and Wednesday Bible studies,
All are good inside themselves,
But all become most evil
When I'm cast upon the shelves.
I'm here right now to lift you up.
It's plain, oh can't you see?
I'm not inside the walls of a church.
No wooden frames hold me.
I've made a home inside your heart.
It's warm, cozy, and free.
All I want is for you to come back
And sit a while with me."

Let's take the time, dear kindred souls,
To rest upon His shoulders.
Let's feast upon His presence's bread,
Instead of gnashing on the world's boulders.
All the sermons in all the world
Will fill us with dismay
If we forget our Savior's near,
No matter what the day.

"I've seen a thousand different churches
With a thousand different names.
All inside are cold as steel
And rot like their wooden frames.
All will turn from dust to dust,
Lest they call upon my name.
All will turn from ash to ash,
Until they call upon my name."

Christ

You

$\mathcal{M}$y favorite part about God is that when the gloves come off and the performance is done, when church is over and the preaching ends and the music stops, you can go right back to Him. When you're exhausted, tired, weary, broken, and tongue-tied, you can ask Jesus to pray for you even if no one else will. After all, that is what He stands before the Father doing eternally (Hebrews 7:25).

When words can't explain
What I want to say,
You still listen to my heart.
When I'm too tired to pray,
You smile when I say,
"You start."

When I can't get out of bed
And am too weary to face the day,
You love me and say, "My son."
When I'm too tired to walk,
You remind me of Your power.
You challenge me and say, "Let's run!"

An Easter Poem

Power in identity
That's borne upon the nail,
Pressure all around me
But bound to never fail,

Power from above
From He who reigns on high,
Daylight in my soul
Though darkness lingers nigh,

Power over sin
Through grace and patient love,
Steadfastness in my holy savior
Though darkness tries to shove,

Unlimited wealth and majesty
My resources in store,
Unlimited peace from suffering,
My Lord forevermore.

One Small Child

Christ repeatedly tells us that it is necessary to have the mind of a child to enter the kingdom of heaven. A practical exercise, then, is to imagine yourself a child upon the knee of the King. It is humbling but necessary to understand that this is part of the proper relationship between Christ and His church. Doing so is also one of His commands. (Matthew 18:3, Mark 10:5).

God of ages,
My rock and sword
Let me stand
By your word.

If I fall,
I cannot stand it,
But you're the way.
For me, you planned it.

My recompense,
My Lord on high,
Let me sit
Upon your thigh.

I'll tell you a joke,
My favorite one.
If I make you smile,
The world I've won.

Here I sit;
I need no other.
Just let me chill
With my older brother.

Take my hand;
Won't you see?
This man is all
You'll ever need.

He loves you more
Than to the moon and back.
He loves you—see
The scars on His back,

Nails in his hands
And in his feet,
So that one day soon
We all can meet,

He and His dad
Enthroned on high?
I pray so hard
That day is nigh.

We'll see Him,
And He'll see us.
We'll be wrapped up in
Eternal trust.

Lord on high,
Hear me below.
I really think
That you should know
That you are loved
Despite my flaws,
That when I don't say it
I still mean it.
I pray my meaning—
I hope you glean it.
I love you much.
Let's keep in touch.

The Giver

$\mathcal{I}$ was in a particularly deep place of depression when this poem came to me. I was praying when I felt the inspiration, and immediately I had to write. This time, the writing itself was the prayer and response.

Who thought a morning fog and tire
Could so easily a prayer inspire?
Like a lame and flightless dove
Trying to reach the heavens above.

Reach down for me and hear my cry!
Why do you let my soul run dry?
Why do I think to only write
When I am feeling so contrite?

Where is my faith and hope so gentle
When I feel confusion mental?
Can you see or can you hear
My inner monologue so filled with fear?

What does it take to get your attention?
What sacred rite do I enact or mention?

Or are you here and tougher than me,
Just hiding in a way I cannot see?

"Pick up your cross." I cannot bear it.
I writhe and wriggle, a dying ferret.
"Pick up your cross and follow me."
Where are we going? I cannot see.

"Pick up your cross. Have faith, my son."
When, and where, will this battle be won?
"Upon your grave and tombstone somber
Is when you'll cease to ever wander
Upon these plains and fetid hills,
Hearing cries that are so shrill,
Of dying souls and spirits a-slumber.
With this in mind, is it a wonder
That my servant David said,
This is the 'valley of the shadow of the dead'?"

So first I die before it's over,
Before I burst forth like a four-leaf clover?
Why must I die before I live?
"This is the gift I came to give.
Where others die, you will ascend
And will your torment finally end.
I feel it too—don't get it twisted.
I sent my spirit. You haven't missed it.
Our souls entwined,
Your pain is mine.
I'm with you till the end of time."

Across the Eastern Sky

7 sat by the window in my bedroom looking out across a winter's night sky. I wanted so dearly for Jesus to come back. My bedroom faces the east, and I remember how Christ described the day of His second coming. It will be swift, like a thief in the night. Suddenly, a whole poem began to flow from my thumbs almost faster than I could type it into my phone. A story of judgment day unfolded before me. It was swift, awkward, and abrupt. Few people were ready for it.

"Lukas, tell me a story
Of your life back on earth,"
A small child called out to me
As she tore across heaven's turf.
"A story again? Well, let's think and see.
Ah yes, I remember, it was a night wintery."

I sat there troubled
By my problems piled high.
Years till then I'd waited,
And now there's a flash 'cross the eastern sky,
A trumpet's song, a clarion call
Across the world renowned.

To some it was life; to others death,
A beautiful, terrible sound.

The sky rolled back, and the earth retreated—
Heaven was opened wide.
The Son of man descended in bright, gleaming glory
With ten thousand angels at His side.
"Come home, my friends. This is the end,
The start of a brand new day.
Through all your trials, all your persecutions,
You've run the entire way."

A million marched home tearful;
A billion passed me by.
I saw some were standing still,
And they began to cry.
"Now you, my less-than-faithful,
Where is your excuse?
Do you still call for hot debate?
Do you still cry out for proof?
Where were you when I was wet,
Sick, lonely, and cold?
Where were you when I was an orphan young,
Or dying, very old?
How is your schedule? How is your self?
Have your ambitions brought you peace?
Do you still wish you looked away
From the worst, and ill, and least?
Where are your riches? Where is your glory?
Did I not make them all?
Where are those on whose shoulders you stood
To make you look so tall?

They're home with me, so you can see
I was all you'd ever need.
While you held them down,
I held them up under the weight of all your greed."

I saw now billions on the plains,
Plainly terrified.
For them, "religious fantasy"
Had finally just arrived.
He walked from man to woman,
Eternity at His toes.
He questioned and He searched
In their hearts and in their souls.
A man in black from head to toe
With boldness more than mine
Reached up high like a schoolchild,
A question on his mind.

And then you, little one, ran and pulled
On glorious Jesus's robes.
With patience and humility,
He bent and touched your nose.

You said, "Excuse me, Jesus, I saw a man.
Looking sad, he raised his hand.
My teacher taught me back in school
That every question deserves a stand."

With a father's smile, He picked you up
And called the man by name.
The man didn't move; the people around him
Withdrew quickly in their shame.

He said, "I'm sorry, Jesus. I'm not that strong.
My words will stammer and not flow,
But all along I wondered deep,
'How are we supposed to know?'
How can we be certain that you're the truth?
You lived so long ago."

A storm brewed up, and fire flew
From the heavens to the earth.
But not a soul moved;
We trembled all beneath the moment and its girth.

I could see a furnace fire
Burning in Jesus's eyes.
The thunderstorm got loud enough
To drown out the people's cries.
It died away and grew deathbed silent;
He still held you in His arms.
The man looked away, didn't know what to say.
We could feel his sense of alarm.
"Come," said God, with the peace of a breeze.
"Come forward, and you will see
Those who bore the burden and cross
Of my gospel testimony."
One by one, there filed out people
Of each and every kind.
Short and tall, all countries, nations,
All types that you could find.

Some women, some men, some children,
But they all shone with glory.
Jesus went down and hugged each one,

Inviting them to tell their story.
Time and again, shamed, beaten, mocked,
The martyrs retold their lives.
They stood against darkness at the ultimate cost
To their loved ones, husbands, or wives.

The martyrs showed their scars and glory,
And finally Jesus showed His:
The holes in His hands, the scars on His back,
And where the Roman's spear pierced His ribs.

"You see, dear child," He turned back to the man,
"It's not like they ever knew either.
Uncertainty plagued them the length of their days,
But they never chose to feed her.
They had their questions and had their doubts,
But you don't need to 'know' to act.
Faith comes by hearing, and you heard a lot
Of their faith and My covenant pact.
So these are the faithful, and now they're my
children, Who carried their crosses with grace."
The man was deeply afflicted;
Paralyzing fear was written across his face.

Jesus stared at the tall man in black,
But His subject just wouldn't look back.
He stammered and trembled and looked out
of place, Until finally his will did crack.
He fell to his knees and uneasily wept,
Screams and sobs the same.
"Jesus, my Lord, why didn't you help me
With my grief and all of my pain?"

Jesus knelt down and looked at the man.
"Was it enough to forsake my name?"

The billions of saved looked in on the scene.
It's happened to you and me—
That harsh and rough prayer when a sinner admits
The journey takes him further than he can see.

"I just couldn't do it. The weight was too much.
I left, I ran, I worried.
I forsook your name because I was scared,
And now you've come back in quite a hurry.
Jesus, I don't get it, but I'm scared of what's next.
Is there a way you'd take me back?
I never got over leaving the path,
And since then I've dressed in black."

The man didn't look up, but if he did he would see
A teary-eyed Jesus staring right back at he.
"Is there a way?" the sobbing man screamed,
Broken and weak in his bones.
Jesus replied, "I am the way! Come
home, my son, come home!"
The man keeled over and wept in the sand.
"My Lord and Savior, my God!"
An angel shrieked in joy, and all the crowd jumped.
"He is worthy of praise and laud!"

A chorus joined in, "Worthy is He!
The maker of all the world!
Worthy is He, the slayer of death,
His glory forever unfurled!"

Jesus picked the man up and called to the
faithless, "Come, if you're weary, to rest!"
A great crowd lined up with their heads hung low;
They were at least a thousand abreast.
But the strange thing was,
Not everyone was in line.
I heard more than one say, "He's no Lord of mine.
We're probably hallucinating; it'll wear off in time."
"So he receives the betrayer?
He's a penchant for abuse."
"I definitely think He has a couple of screws loose."
"If God was really real, He'd make us believe."
I cried, "And still you do not,
With all that you've seen?!"
"Well, stress and such factors
Cause one's brain to malfunction.
It'd be foolish to make a conclusion
Here at this junction."
Then I heard my name called by that beautiful voice.
"Quickly!" I begged them. "You must make a choice!"
"Lukas!" I heard, and on His face I saw sadness.
"You cannot help them.
They've chosen their madness."
"But you—" I whimpered.
"I can't make them do it.
If they don't grab my hand,
I can't help them through it."

We both turned in sadness, His arm on my shoulder.
The weight of lost souls hung on me like a boulder.
"A choice must be made between Me and the world.
This was the plan before time was uncurled."

I nodded in agreement and faced my new family,
Saints dressed in white as far as the eye could see.
The pain and weight of life on earth was now lost,
But the scars on His hands reminded me of the cost.
Now, between laughs, I see that light in His eye.
It brings me back to that wintery night
And the flash 'cross the eastern sky.

Printed in the United States
By Bookmasters